RHYMES THAT ROCK

Poems for Everyone

DR RAKESH PATIL

BookLeaf Publishing

India | USA | UK

Made with ❤ on the BookLeaf Publishing Platform
www.bookleafpub.in
www.bookleafpub.com

Dedication

This book is dedicated to every person who has a love for language and literature. In this today's world of learn to earn , very few people are able to pursue their love for literature. Simply because , it needs a kind of disconnect from the materialistic world to gain insights into your creative aspects which many are unable to do so. Hoping this book will add to your library and inspire many such hidden potential poets all over. And those already pursuing their love for literature, I hope this book brings a smile to their face which will give me the necessary impetus for future ahead.

Preface

It gives me great pleasure to present everyone my first ever publication. This book has 21 poems on different topics . I have tried to share my view point and experiences .. My love for poetry & language exists right from my school days. I was very fond of Grammar and still I am a grammar Nazi , for which many of my peers get irritated. I have tried to use my poetic liberties in this book to the fullest.

I feel every thought should be penned down to avoid mental over crowding. In todays world we all are short of time.. But its all about priorities I feel, nobody is too busy. So pursue that artistic side of yours, whatever it be like I just did. So basically , I took up this challenge of writing 21 poems in 21 days .. At first I was little skeptical. but later just went along with the flow .. and I think it was totally worth it in the end .

I am open to all your feedback and opinions ..
Please reach out to me what you liked and what
you did not.. On an ending note I will say..

" A moment of silence, and a little bit of
time
Every thought of yours can turn into a
rhyme"

Dr Rakesh K Patil

Acknowledgements

*I acknowledge the support by my family in
writing this book and explore my poetic side
Poem on books is inspired by my daughters love
for books.
The one poem on chess for my son who is a
chess prodigy already at young age
My wife for constant encouragement .
My late younger brother whom i miss till today.
My parents and friends
who have shaped me into the human being I am
today
My profession as a doctor which I value the
most. My schooling days where I learnt English
and was obsessed about poetic brilliance
And finally bookleaf for allowing me to
challenge myself to express my poetic liberties*

1. Digital De-addiction : Need of the hour

*The world seems smaller today, thanks to technology
and innovation
We can reach out to each & everyone, in this age of
digital telecommunication
Virtual Chats and DM's have replaced the age old meet &
greet in person
But such is our dependence on these modalities, as if
they are oxygen*

*This virtual world at our fingertips has created a lot of
mayhem & chaos
From adults facing sleep issues, to teenagers befriending
foes
We know more about distant people, than about those
living close.
And then in case of any emergency or help needed, we
are all left alone*

We are so much used to typing, have forgotten our own

handwriting

Virtual world has made us forget ,the real world battles
we were fighting
From Knowledge seeking to attention craving, our kids
IQ is declining
Once virtuous and innocent kids, today their inner
demons are biting

We have just evolved from usage to habit, from habit to
addiction
Without these things today, we will suffer even in our
imagination
Once proud masters, we are now becoming slaves to our
own inventions
Digital de-addiction is the need of the hour ,to salvage
this generation

2. The World of Chess

A mocktail of imagination and calculation,
A cocktail of attack and defense ,
Nothing is random or inappropriate here ,
Even a mistake has to make some sense

Victory gives you pride and appreciation
Defeat elevates your level through vengeance
Its an exercise for your brain like no other
Welcome to the amazing world of chess

A cold war fought over 64 squares battleground,
Every move matters here, the flying queen or steady
pawn
Every piece is important, their positioning profound
You need to learn the trades , from dusk till dawn

Its a war without bloodshed dear , but drains you like
hell
A moment you thought are on top, next moment your
kingdom fell

*Sometimes you lose without doing much wrong, there is
nobody to tell
Sometimes.. you win with ease and the whole world is
left to dwell*

*White or black piece you play , your game needs to be
precise
e4 , d4 , Italian or English .. these openings are a
common exercise
Fork, gambit , pin or skewer can make any opponent
pressurize
And endgame is the crux, like a phoenix from ashes you
can rise*

*From rookie to master then to grandmaster the journey
is turbulent
Only for a few brilliant minds , these titles are truly
meant..
Locally to globally , you need to conquer all the
tournament..
For those who finally make it to top , its a glorious
achievement..*

3. BOOKS .. The companions for life

Of all the hobbies one has to pursue ,
Book reading is the one I will surely recommend you
Blessed are those readers very intelligent few
Unlocking regions of their brains so new

Open a book and a mystery unravels in our mind ,
To all our unsolved questions , answers we find
We become more aware of problems facing mankind.
We start seeing things clearly, to which we were initially blind

Reading calms your mind, as if you visit a shrine
It won't erase troubles, but you will surely feel fine
Binge read a book , just leave that web-series online
Find the difference , see what adds to your spine

Lots of crap on the Internet , books offer quality for our brains to feed
They give you such company , no other friend you need

*Books add more to your personality , than any other
deed
Kudos to today's book readers , tomorrow's world you
will lead*

4. Life cycle of a medico

After topping charts in school & colleges in oblivion,
Our dreams soar high ,we are high on energy & ambition
And then a selected few shine & rise above the
competition.
On cloud number 9 , we enter this esteemed profession

Enter medical college, we learn so much amazing stuff
But soon the never ending syllabus gives us a bad cough
And soon we feel, our high scores in school were a bluff
Even spending the entire night studying is not enough

And our amazing seniors take us on a journey we dread
Some call it ragging , for some it's nothing but
enrichment
It teaches us things, books will never teach us instead
Coz destiny is never easy ,tougher paths we need to
tread..

Somehow we clear this phase and level up next ,
We seek companionship & develop new friends

And off course there is always the one of the opposite
sex
With whom we seek our chemistry to be the best

It's an amalgamation of many firsts in our life
First failure, first night out , first drinks , first fight
We learn to be confident in whatever worst may arise
Also.. We learn to be carefree in tense moments with
pride

Somehow we clear all hurdles & cross the finish line
We feel blessed , brighter than ever on us the sunshine
Our once messy outlook ,soon starts appearing fine
We thank our parents & teachers & bow down before the
divine

Then comes internship, we tune into patient universe
We follow nurses orders, for in future our roles reverse
We learn that round the clock work is not that worse
Also, it's the first time , we have our own money in
purse

This final frontier is nothing short of conquering a fort
For the convocation day , our best possible look we sport
Wearing a smile with black hat & black overcoat ,
To serve the mankind we take the Hippocrates Oath

5. The Right One

The one who overcame all obstacles with grace and
finesse
Amidst all adversities, he followed the path of
righteousness
His virtues and values still relevant in today's world full
of mess
He is the one and only Lord Shri Ram ,we bow down to
his highness

A re-incarnation like no other, so blessed was our planet
earth.
It was 5000 years ago , the eldest son of King Dashratha
took his birth
Ayodhyaa kingdom of yesterday, today houses a
magnificient temple in its girth..
It was the Treta Yuga , Lord Ram began his journey to
prove his worth

Polite words and graceful demeanour , he enchanted the
masses all over

Justice for the needy, punishment for the greedy were
his endeavour
His love for parents and siblings alike always etched in
his heart forever
He was a true preacher of goodness, the world will
always remember

Todays gen Z astonished by Mjolnir lifted by an
imaginary God Thor,
To be worthy of lifting the famous Lord Parshuram bow,
is not just a folklore
Lord Ram proved his fortitude and greatness by winning
the contest
The Eternal love of Lord Ram and Goddess Sita , nobody
can manifest

Every living being on this planet has to suffer and Lord
Ram was no exception,
To fulfil his step mother's wish and a previous life curse
he went into extinction
Lord Ram accepted 14 years vanvaas with grace and
absolutely no hesitation,
With Goddess Sita and brother Laxman by his side ,
began the expedition

Feeding on raw fruits and vegetables, facing
environmental hazards all along,

Lord Ram won hearts wherever he went , and not a foot
he put was wrong,
Then came mighty Ravan and abducted Goddess Sita
with trickery & deception,
He wasn't aware whom he has troubled, and the after
effects , the repercussion

Lord Ram set on the path to fight the evil with all his
might and vengeance
Lord Hanuman and a battalion of apes , joined forces and
gave assistance
To reach Lanka was not easy, it was a golden island
amidst the ocean
With the chants of Lord Ram ,in no time a floating bridge
of stones was woven

And then the battle ensued , between right and the
wrong, good and the evil.
Lord Ram prevailed supreme and killed Ravan saving
Goddess Sita from peril
After 14 years, in Ayodhyaa lights and diyas lit up to
welcome Lord Ram,
We celebrate Diwali this day, symbolizing victory of
brightness over the dark..

6. Life Cycle Of a Doctor

*After 6 long years of patience and perseverance, finally
doctors we become,*
*Unsure of what lies ahead, yet we are happy with a
moment of stardom*
*Our parents are over the moon.. as if they could
broadcast to entire nation*
*Peers feel like we conquered everest , but ahead lies trial
and tribulation*

*Some start studying for further specialities , some happy
to start their own clinic*
*Some happy to serve bond in rural areas, some join any
hospital for apprentice*
*This is when we learn art of prescription, and the art of
comforting and healing ,*
*To relieve patients of their discomfort ,is like a
superpower & the best feeling*

*Initial days are tough for a novice, lot of apprehensions
and self doubts arise,*

*Will my patient feel better with medicines? ,such
thoughts run through our minds.
Its a science after all, and not some magic or a fluke
,soon we realize
This is when we feel , we are worthy of the title doctor
and start the exercise*

*Slowly our patient flow increases, and we gain
acceptance from the vicinity
Our personality also glitters now, with limelight comes
decency and dignity
We grow in stature and are more confident and mature
in our words we speak
We receive praise and appreciation, feels maybe we are
now at our peak..*

*However, a pandemic like COVID occurs and disrupts
our assumption..
There is a super power above us, everthing occurs under
his jurisdiction
We treat he cures, is what we always need to understand
and remember
For some patients will experience January, some will feel
its December*

*Yet we devote so much time to strangers, our families we
hardly meet*

New clinics, new equipments keep coming , new
vacation takes a backseat
Work life balance is a concept easy to talk about, difficult
to establish
Its not like a fish without water here, rather a matter of
water without fish ..

That doesn't imply we hate our profession , just the
sacrifices are more
We detach from our personal side most of the times,
amidst all the chore
Even we are vulnerable human beings , can have some
fallacies , some flaws
Always under the camera lens , ready to pounce on us
are societal claws

In these difficult times , lets protect and unite together all
our doctor fraternity,
For a society to understand a doctor's dilemma , will take
an eternity
Avoid jousting or false claims , rather work hard to the
best of your ability
As Peter Parker once said, "With great power comes
great responsibilty"

7. The Secret Of Mine

*It was a cold evening in paris.. On a secret mission I
checked into a hotel
A drug mafia and his gang were staying in room 1006 ,
as per the intel
All came to meet a drug distributor there ,. drugs to
whom they could sell
They had never seen him before , so I planned to instead
disguise myself*

*I neutralized the distributor in the hotel spa and took
away his phone
Opened the phone with his fingerprints and all the data I
could restore
Knowing about 12 odd languages I could speak in fluent
French tone
I called the drug mafia from that phone and told him to
meet me alone*

*He agreed to meet in the hotel cafeteria at midnight in
silence*

*We both confirmed our identities, and discussed the
trade in depth*
*I showed him the trading routes & probable points of
police interference*
*He seemed more relaxed now, with my experience I
could impress*

*We talked over a deal, I told I would first like to see the
consignment*
*He agreed and showed me the drugs kept in the hotel
basement*
*I was overpowered and handcuffed by him to my
astonishment*
*He said he was an undercover cop and to catch me was
his assignment*

*There broke my dream, and I started laughing in shock
and bewilderment ,*
*An undercover cop catching another undercover cop,is
too much to comprehend*
*A script worthy of a spy movie , in my dream I was able
to act and implement*
*Such dreams are a rarity , where we are left feeling if in
reality it could happen*

*Actually, there is a secret of mine deep within today I
will like to share ,*

I wished I could be a spy since childhood .. my
whereabouts, nobody aware
I could have multiple passports and currencies , the
world would be my fair,
Every moment unpredictable, every move suspicious , I
won't really care

8. Flashback to a day I spent in COVID times

Not a good time for us to be living in today
Not a single soul can say I am feeling okay
Once clear skies , now filled with clouds grey
Once filled with hope we are now in dismay

Humanity gripped with uncertainty and fear
Search for hope everywhere, far and near
Occasions to rejoice , no longer we cheer
There aint no filter , the only good we could hear

Pandemic has spared no one, struggles all over
Beds and medicines difficult to procure..
Difficulty in breathing has never been so severe
Breaking bad news, breaking us more than ever.

Covid warriors we are but, now limited armour
We spend sleepless nights, trying to be saviour
To overcome the eventuality is our endeavour

*Human beings we are, if you rejoice our success, also
understand our failure..*

*Sincere apologies if I cant update u again & again.
I am busy standing there with umbrella protecting you
from rain
Sincere apologies today if I cant pick up your call
I will be there to pick you up in case you fall*

*Sincere apologies if i cant arrange you a bed
A thousand eventualities going through my head
Sincere apologies if I cant get you medicines
If I had that privilege, why would i be so tense*

*The world is in need of mercy & common sense much
more than ever..
We all are mere mortals , clever or unclever
Dont say we are spared, it will happen never
Prepare and protect yourself ,whomsoever*

*Maybe we cannot take anything granted in life
For a seed you planted just yesterday, fruits won't
immediately ripe
Nothing is easy, everything hangs on the edge of knife
This phase should soon pass, don't let the memories and
learnings wipe*

9. Re-unions , pure bliss

*Re-unions are truly magical , the good old times we can
remember*
*Our long lost friends we meet , we can re-live the past
together*
*So just plan that re-union whenever you can , do make
that endeavour*
*Bcoz life gives limited opportunities to enjoy, its now or
never*

*Re-unions are also an opportunity for some people to
shine*
*Those in the yesteryears lackluster ,may turn out now in
their prime*
*It's a wonderful party , to dance and celebrate , to wine
and dine*
*It's also a moment to re-kindle the chemistry , which
faded with time*

*It's a competition sometimes to see who is still in best of
the shape*

*Some lose their hair and charm , while some gifted ones
just don't age
Some show off their achievements with pride , some
show humility & grace
Some become more notorious than before , some turn
into a sage*

*We shared our golden years together, we shared a
beautiful past,
Re-unions can add a plethora of new memories, all can
have a blast
Time will soon catch up with everyone and all ,either
slow or fast
Everyone be left with nothing really ,except for our their
own shadows to cast*

10. Unknown Battles

*It's easy to judge someone and think they can't do
anything right
But remember , even the darkest cloud has a silver lining
bright
Some fly high some stay low , for some it's day , some
it's night
Some have just started climbing , some have reached the
height*

*We might feel someone is blessed and his life is full of
flare
But he may be fighting battles unknown , the world is
unaware
Show some mercy & acceptance ,show remorse and care
Don't just jump to conclusions, and think the world is
unfair*

*Let's stop prejudice and bias , stop having pre conceived
notions
Accept people as they are , be true to your deeds and*

intentions
Work hard to build trust in relations, leaving aside
assumptions.
Build strong friendships , beyond economic and social
recognitions

Everybody has their own story ,nobody else knows
Everybody has ups in life ,and everybody has lows
Nobody can know you more than yourself, be it far or
close
Because nobody can tread the river that through your
mind flows

11. We will Re-unite

I knew you had to leave someday
I ignored this fact, it felt very grey
I am an atheist, I did never pray
I feel sad and disheartened today

Felt the tide will never me disfavour
That you shall keep up your endeavour
And your company will betray me never
But we mortals are not so clever

I have achieved a penny lost a pound
I feel so insecure now, my mind unsound
Hence I cry out to the winds surround
How on earth will solace be found ?

You disappeared, No good-bye
You conquered hearts, minds alike
In the parallel universe, now you lie
Your soul so pure, your enemies too cry

You shall find a world more beautiful
You shall meet people more wonderful
Your memories we will cherish till end of time
Your goodwill has taught many the meaning of life

At infinity may be, we shall meet
Our roles reverse, I touch your feet
Today time outran us, such a cheat
To my grief, hope the divine pays heed

I had my dreams, with you by my side
Friends so few, coz in you I confide
In this mortal universe so infinite
We will re-unite ...we will re-unite..

12. The Rock Dynasty

Long ago in 10th century .. ruled Rock the emperor
mighty & courageous
He was a true leader , ruthlesss to enemies, to people he
was generous
He was energetic and enigmatic , his goodwill very
infectious
His kingdom was envied by many , even his friends were
jealous

It was a magnificent kingdom for real ,and not a green
screen gimmick
Amazing piece of architecture, awesome in every sense
with perfect finish
Every inhabitant was blessed & prosperous ,in good
health and not sick
It was built by the people themselves , all the walls and
pillars ,every piece of brick

Many invaders came and went , but all their efforts went
in vain,

His troops were the best in combat , for all enemies
suffering in pain,
It was just not muscle and power , the Rock dynasty also
put in their brain
Even for the mightiest of attackers , not an inch of land
anybody could gain

But all good things have to fall , and indeed this was not
an exception
A Turkish king came to befriend emperor Rock, after
seeking permission
He poisoned all his court personnel with some magical
potion
He held the emperor captive and imprisoned him in his
own mansion

Emperor Rock was freed by his people and in a cave he
took hostage,
The Turkish king started searching, full of anguish and
full of rage
Inside the cave the emperor found a mirror and guess
what he could gaze ?
He could see an image of himself but in different clothes
not belonging to his age

It was me at the other end of the magical mirror seeing
my previous life

Many familiar faces which I see in today's world i could recognize
Why I am nicknamed Rock in this life, it's definitely now not a surprise
Continuing my previous life legacy, I find fun in now captivating minds

13. The Love Of My life

To love someone is a feeling you cant just express in
words or phrase
Some stranger before, now occupies in your heart most
prized place
its an emotion, an ecstasy, and its a vital component of
your happy space
True love stays relevant even today, no situationship or
fling can replace

Indeed I was lucky in my yester-years to meet the love of
my life
Our love blossomed, I am lucky enough she happens to
be my wife
She is with me always , through good and bad , easy or
tough time
She is the most important reason today why any thought
of mine can rhyme..

She is a simplistic woman , a calming influence for my
mind

*I am the one restless & chirping, she is sorted and sober
all the time*
*I am in disbelief how she accepted me, my destiny to me
was so kind.*
*Many wrong ones I fell for in despair, before the right
one i could find*

*We have our own share of quarrels too, nothing there to
lie*
*But we are so fond of each other ,that soon our anger
will die*
*She understands my insecurities and also if am not
happy why*
*She is the reason why even if adversity., I can still afford
to smile*

*She appreciates the good in everyone always, a quality
very difficult to acquire*
*She enjoys true fan following and meaningful
friendships which I truly admire*
*She is a trend setter of her own kind, you cant copy her
but for many to inspire*
*She is like ice for those who are nice, but for those who
trouble her she is fire*

*And yet she feels I am stupid ,could have easily dated &
married a better woman*

Only I know how lucky I am, without her my life would
be grave and no real fun
She makes me a better person today.. I acknowledge
,from her a lot I could learn
I must have done something good in my previous life for
a love like this to earn..

14. Debunking Success

It's not just a matter of fluke or throw of a dice
Need to work hard consistently, to win the prize
Need to have patience, high or low be the tide
In troubled waters, your ship needs to survive

Pounce on every opportunity, don't close ur eyes.
Time is like a river, it flows forward with no rewind
You may fail again & again, once, twice or thrice
Self doubts and despair should never in your mind arise

Millions are running, only few touch the finish line
Losers feel shattered & sick, as if end of life
But winners only know what they had to sacrifice
Success is not anyone's cup of tea, we fail to realize

Enjoy the journey till it lasts, let destiny whenever
finally arrive
Celebrate the newer version of you, and what all you had
to survive
Some peak early, some late.. so just concentrate on your

own timeline
Start ploughing your own yard, Grass is not always
greener on the other side

15. Exams , A Blessing In Disguise

Schooling years are the best , we acquire skills and new
things we learn
We enjoy social interaction with peers and also many
friends we earn
We engage in group tasks and extra curricular activities
are so much fun
Many of us however feel the heat and pressure when
eventually exams happen

Some excel in flying colours , some are midway while
some at the bottom ,
Not all fingers are same , for some it's an ecstasy , for
some it's boredom
Never skip any exam though , just for a false sense of
freedom
Maybe you are destined to succeed later in life , only
time will tell you the dictum

Exams are necessary to know your standings in the

competition
Exams are necessary to stamp some authority on your
ambition
Don't think you can skip an exam , thinking you don't
need adjudication
Life itself is an exam dear, tougher roads are waiting in
apprehension

Indeed you need to be prepared for anything and
everything in life
Problem solving skills is the need of the hour than hiding
yourself in archive
Exams create the necessary anxiety to strengthen &
sharpen your mind
They bring out the best in you indeed , Exams are a like
blessing in disguise

16. Global Warming , an imminent threat

Amidst the scorching heat, we pray for a gush of cold
little breeze
We take shelter and seek comfort in the soothing shade
of trees
These trees we are cutting down for monetary gains &
selfish needs
The greenery is declining now and so is the IQ and the
peace

We conserve our own energy and burn the fuel
inadvertently
Discontinuing ancestral active lifestyle ,we have become
sedentary
We shop for fun, clothes or toys beyond limits of
necessity
We are just leaving our carbon footprints which last till
eternity

Summers are getting hotter than before ,it's not just a

mere co-incidence
Flooding of areas that never flooded before, due to
urbanisation so dense
The glaciers are melting and rise in sea levels is now so
immense
We fear in few years many cities will vanish underwater
beyond any lens

Our timely actions today will shape the tomorrow of our
future generation
Plant more trees and save fuel, our planet needs our
support and appreciation
Act responsibly and adopt renewable energy sources
whatever indication
The ball is in our court , choose wisely between salvation
or annihilation

17. Now or Never

There is no perfect time or a juncture to do something in
life
So better put your plans to action now or else time will
just fly
There is still an order to all random happenings occuring
all the while
Things will fall in place eventually, but don't just sit idle,
give it a try..

The same phase of life you wish will come never back
again
All the emotions you experience will reshape you,
whether joy or pain
Enjoy every moment to its fullest, don't shut the door ,
don't refrain
Give your heart some ears too , don't just listen to your
brain

Aiming for a better future we toil hard, week in week
out ,night or day

But certain things lose the spark once the right time has passed away
So start living in the present, and be prepared for come what may
In the blue skies of life , there will be occasional clouds of grey

So Take the plunge ,and let it happen , don't sit and wonder
Let the lighting strike the earth, don't wait for the thunder
Make such beautiful memories , a lifetime to remember
Never say can I or should I , coz age is just a number

18. Our daughter , our lifeline

It was the end of a long summer and monsoon was soon
going to arrive
With tiny little feet and shrill cries , a cute little angel
entered our lives
I saw her and felt so blessed, I was happy & ecstatic on
cloud number nine
I kissed my wife and with tears of joy we bowed down
before the divine

She sat & crawled , stood and walked.. slowly she now
started to speak
Her musical voice enchanted our ears, her actions &
expressions for our eyes a treat
We named her after Goddess Saraswati, from her
blessings we always seek
Many parents must have prayed to God, but we are
happy the criteria we could meet ..

She is kind and considerate to her peers , loving and
affectionate
Her enigma and aura ..the world gets attracted to , she
acts like a magnet
Studious and smart.. her brain is far superior , she
doesn't need a gauntlet
She is the perfect rainbow of our life , and not just
shades of scarlet or velvet

She is the perfect host & a natural fashionista, never
taught her a thing about it
She is a natural caretaker for younger kids around , she
can in fact babysit
She is not bothered anymore if the world is jealous of
her, blessed with such wit
She is too mature & wise for a 11 year old , many grown
ups also can't with her compete

Books are her favorite companions, in contrast to today's
screen addicted generation
Her happiness is unparalleled and unbound, inside books
she finds salvation
She dances like a diva with those talkative eyes, holding
the world in captivation
In todays fake and materialistic world, in friends and
family she finds satisfaction

*She will grow up to be a beautiful soul , she already is in
our eyes
She will be flag bearer of truth and honesty , no
deception ,no lies
May Lord be kind and give her the opportunity to serve
the mankind ..
As long as we live , we will stand by her always.. our
daughter , our lifeline*

19. The Obsession for Abroad

In search of better paychecks and quality of living, many flock overseas
Amazed by the advances and comforts, they are all very happy and at ease
Soon establishing own identity at workplace, and staying at homes on lease
After crossing many hurdles and struggles, finally their minds are at peace

Everyone is a stranger there.. some are helpful and caring, some are indifferent
Some welcome with open arms ,some feel there country for you is not meant
Inadvertently, significant years of life of immigrants on foreign lands are spent
Families are left behind in homeland, only source of emotion will be 1-2 friends

On many auspicious occasions, to visit family & friends

they cant visit homeland
To progress ahead in career and life , they will have to
take such tough stand
Healthcare facilities are top notch there but protocols not
easy to understand
Unlike our country India where doctors are just a phone
call away to attend

Local well wisher grocery shop owner replaced by fat
bearded supermart guy
Traffic rules may land you in prison.. if you are not alert
all over cameras will spy
Ever changing government policies will make you
restless & sometimes cry
But somehow they adapt.. because now not going back is
a matter of false pride

You can accumulate a fortune there guys , but remember
what all you have to sacrifice
Parents left all alone to age away in despair is not what
our culture and traditions comprise
Be ambitious.. but serve own country first where
freedom fighters have laid down their lives
Materialistic world , materialistic thoughts are not
enough, you need a clear conscience to survive

20. Friends

Once strangers , now important part of our lives with them we share
We don't meet them often , but there is always a sense of emotion & care,
In today's crowd of judgemental people , they offer a breath of fresh air
Friends are our kindest blessings.. come what may, they are always there

They are selfless and kind ,and give support to our goals and ambition
They provide love and compassion , in this unforgiving world of competition
We can chill with them , and meet our own self beyond any jurisdiction
They act like a catalyst to express ourself , leaving aside inhibition

However big be the problem, friends offer a stupid but easy solution

*Our apprehensions and fear no more , all meet their end
point dilution*
*Their presence like oxygen amidst the environment full
of pollution*
*With them by our side ,all our worries and troubles soon
find resolution*

*Smile we do always but we actually laugh when we are
with friends*
*They roast us badly sometimes , which we enjoy and
take no offence*
*Beyond societal & monetary gains, friendships carry so
much significance*
*They are like a back up, standing when it matters
whatever be circumstance*

*So make those plans to catch up with your friends, new
or old*
*In scorching & tiring heat of life, they provide a sense of
cold*
*Friendships are organic entity , they can't be bought,
can't be sold*
*No amount of money can make you rich , if you have no
friends to behold*

21. Family

*Connected by blood , genetics & a strong bond of
emotions
In every home, a family exists with rich cultural heritage
& traditions
It is indeed our most prized asset , our most sacred
possession
Our heart is where our family is, its not an option but an
obligation*

*We can't stay aloof for long, love is the glue that keeps
us together.
If we are feeling low , just a small chat with our parents
and we feel better ,
Parents provide shelter like no other, amidst the stormy
weather
They are our cheerleaders for life , for them nothing else
will matter*

*Every family is special and unique , be it a joint one or
nuclear*

Spouse and kids are our core component, close to our heart and very very dear
Siblings and cousins may go however far, but always feel near
Uncles and aunts always there to encourage us, we have nothing to fear

For the tree of our life , family are our roots that give us nourishment
They are our constant source of light and hope in the darkest of environment
Families are selfless in their efforts, they don't need any acknowledgement
They are the pinnacle of trust & love , and the highest level of commitment

www.ingramcontent.com/pod-product-compliance
Lightning Source LLC
LaVergne TN
LVHW021250200726
843509LV00012B/1629